HOME SAFETY

Printed in the United States of America.

Library of Congress Cataloging-in-Publication Data
Loewen, Nancy, 1964-
Home Safety/Nancy Loewen.
p.   cm.
Includes bibliographical references.
Summary: Offers basic rules for what to do and what not to
do to be safe at home.
ISBN 1-56766-257-9   (hc : lib. bound)
1. Home accidents --Prevention--Juvenile literature.
2. Safety education--Juvenile literature. [1. Accidents. 2. Safety]
I. Title.
TX150.L64   1996
643'.028'9--dc20   95-25885
CIP
AC

HOME SAFETY

By Nancy Loewen   Illustrated by Penny Dann

THE CHILD'S WORLD

We spend a lot of time in our homes. That's where we eat, sleep, play, work, bathe, entertain friends, and do many other things! But because we do so many things in our homes, we're also at risk for accidents. That's why it's important to know and follow the basic safety rules. Pickles and Roy will show you what to do—and what not to do—to be safe and sound at home!

To prevent falls.

Don't climb or jump on furniture. If you feel you must climb or jump, ask to go to the playground instead!

If you make a mess, clean it up right away. Wipe up any-thing that spills on the floor so you won't slip. And put your toys away so you won't trip. Be especially careful on stairways.

If your home has a **balcony** or deck, don't play on the railing. It's there to prevent you from falling.

Put a rubber mat in the tub, and a **nonskid** rug just outside it. Take care not to slip.

To prevent burns.

Don't play with matches, lighters, candles, or anything else that could start a fire.

Don't touch a hot stove, grill, or heater, and never play with the controls. Don't wear floppy clothing around these things, either. Floppy clothes can catch on fire.

If your parents let you to help with the cooking, make sure you keep the pot handles turned to the back of the stove. That's so no one will knock the hot pans over. Always keep your mind on what you're doing—don't get **distracted**.

Be very **cautious** when using hot water. If it gets too hot,
it could burn you.

Don't use anything sharp unless an adult is there to help you. That goes for kitchen tools such as knives and can openers, and garden tools such as **hoes**, **spades**, and rakes. Put these items away when they're not being used, and store them with the sharp edges turned away.

Don't knock on glass windows or doors, and don't throw anything at or near them. Stay clear of broken glass.

To prevent getting an electric shock.

Water and electricity don't mix. Never use radios, hair dryers or other electrical **appliances** around water, and don't touch them with wet hands.

Don't touch electrical **outlets**—with your fingers or anything else!

Pull on the plug, not the cord, when unplugging an electrical device. Avoid overloading outlets with too many cords.

Many household products are **poisonous**. They should
be stored in a safe place, where children can't get at them.

Medicines that make you feel better when you're sick can be poisonous if you take too much of them or use them the wrong way. Take them only with an adult's **supervision**. Don't eat any plants either. Many common indoor and outdoor plants are poisonous.

To prevent other serious injuries.

Plastic bags aren't toys. You can't breathe through plastic, so stay away from them!

Refrigerators, freezers, or trunks don't make good hiding places, even if there's nothing in them. If you crawl inside, you might not be able to get out again.

Guns are extremely dangerous and should be locked up
at all times. But if you do find a gun, don't touch it.
Instead, tell an adult to put it away in a safe place.

Sometimes emergencies happen no matter how careful you are, so be sure to keep a list of emergency phone numbers by the phone. Know how to give your name, address, and telephone number.

Practice good safety sense and help make your home a safer place to live, work, and play!

Glossary

appliance (a-PLY-ance)
a household or office device. Never use electrical appliances around water.

balcony (BELL-cah-nee)
a platform that extends from a wall or building. If your home has a balcony, don't play on it.

cautious (CAW-tious)
being careful in an action to avoid risk. Be very cautious when using hot water.

distracted (diss-TRACK-tid)
to turn your attention away from one interest to another. When cooking food on the stove, don't get distracted.

hoe (HO)
a tool for mixing or raking. Don't use a hoe unless an adult is there to help you.

nonskid (non-SKID)
designed to prevent slipping. A nonskid rug in the bathroom helps prevent accidents.

outlet (OUT-let)
a place for the plug of an electrical device. Avoid overloading outlets with too many cords.

poisonous (POI-zen-es)
harmful to your health. Many household products are poisonous.

spade (SPADE)
a tool used for digging. Don't use a spade without an adult's help.

supervision (soup-er-VISH-on)
to have direction, being in charge. Don't take medicine without an adult's supervision.